LARF YOUR HEADS OFF

First Published and Illustrated by
Frances Felton
2009

Printed and published by Leiston Press.

Unit 1b, Masterlord Industrial Estate,
Leiston, Suffolk, IP16 4JD
Tel. 01728 833 003
http://www.leistonpress.com

ISBN 978-0-9562896-5-0

Contents Page

Acknowledgment
Acknowledgements are given for the kind permission to use
the company brand names of the following:
Société des produits Nestlés S.A. for the use of the brand
name ROWNTREES
Tesco Stores Ltd, Cheshunt, Hertfordshire EN8 9SL for the
use of the trademark 'TESCO'
Sainsbury's Supermarkets Ltd for the use of the Sainsbury's
name and trademark.

Thank you
I would like to say a big thank you to my friend Brian who has
been my 'proof listener' and my grand-daughter, Sophie, who
did all the computer work for me.

Introduction

Frances Felton has been a volunteer fund raiser for Cancer Research U.K. for 12 years. Writing poetry has been her hobby for the past 35 years.

Frances recently composed a poem to read to guests at her 70th birthday party, it was very well received.

Frances raised £700 for Cancer Research at the party, and was encouraged to publish this book in the hope it can benefit cancer research U.K in the future.

WARNING

To be read at your own risk.

The author and publisher totally disclaim responsibility for any adverse effects that may arise after reading this publication. I.e.: Jaw ache, stomach stitch, headache etc.

If any of these symptoms occur, stop reading immediately, visit your nearest library, and alleviate reaction by reading a serious, sensible book.

Hopefully you will have enjoyed this brief therapy and may become addicted. If this is the case, please read as many times as necessary to achieve the NHS⋆ effect.

⋆ **N**ice **H**appy **S**mile

Date with the Dentist

Yesterday I had a toothache, it drove me nigh insane
I'd lost the cavity filling, and had excruciating pain.

My dentist tried to ease it with his usual 'chair-side' charm
He gave me an injection, to try to make me calm.

I was laid back in the treatment room, blinded by the glare
Of the piercing ultra-violet light, above the dentist chair.

He said 'now open wide,' I thought I've got lock jaw
He put the drill inside my mouth, I couldn't take much
more.

It only took a minute, but it felt more like an hour
You have to thank technology, that drill had so much
power.

When I went to pay the bill, my chin just hit the floor
My pain went to my pocket, and made me feel quite poor.

But at least my smile is confident; I can grin from ear to ear
I can cross the dentist off my list, at least until next year.

I won't eat chocolate anymore, life is full of sacrifices
No sweets, no cakes, no jellybeans, are there any other
vices?

Oh yes, there's one that I forgot, it makes my cheeks go red
But I'm too old in the tooth to practice now,
I'm afraid I'd fall out of bed!

Take Two

This is the story of a man who had charm
He was well known in his profession
He attended church quite regularly
And one day he made a confession.

He was a qualified surgeon
Very confident using a knife
He claimed he had never made a mistake
Never threatened anyone's life.

Sometimes he got very tired
This caused him to get confused
Hence this little poem
Which I hope will keep you amused.

So it was on one of these days
When he'd been working far too long
Everything that he did
Seemed to go horribly wrong.

We all know what young ladies are like
Always maintaining their figure
Well, one day a film star turned up
And requested her bust be made bigger.

The next day another came in
Who wanted some length off her nose
He said he would willingly operate
And agreed with the one that she chose.

He commenced operating on patient one
Mistakenly using the suction
Instead of enhancing her bust line
She ended up with a reduction.

Then patient number two was brought in
And he stretched her nose up to the sky
She was a double of little Pinocchio
After he had told a lie.

Of course, they sued him in court
They had paid him an arm and a leg
He had to admit his mistake
And fell to his knees to beg.

He knelt now, in the confession box
Clutching the bible in his fist
But it didn't convince the priest
He's been struck off the surgeons list.

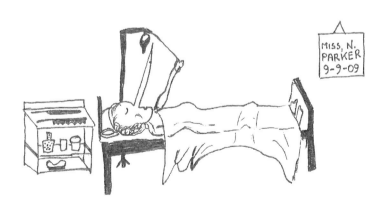

MISS, N.
PARKER
9-9-09

Tommy Rot

I was just a little tomato
Growing on a plot
When a caterpillar came along
And fancied me a lot.

He said 'you look delicious'
Come to my allotment bed'
Then he got his teeth in me
Boy, did I go red.

He said 'you're really tasty'
'Just the thing I needed'
'But I would have liked you even more
If you had been de-seeded'.

Then he just abandoned me
Waved goodbye and grinned
My future looks quite dismal now
I guess I'll end up tinned.

Groupies Lament

I went out one night
And met a bloke who played the drums
I thought that sounded great
Couldn't wait to tell my chums.

He said he had a gig booked
At a hot night club
And invited me to join him
Instead of going to the pub.

So I raked my dancing shoes out
And a mini skirt
I wore them twenty years ago
When I used to flirt.

I toddled to the venue
And was in for a surprise
The queue went round the corner
I could not believe my eyes.

D
e
r
e
k

All the guys looked trendy
The girls were done up to the nines
I was glad I had thick make-up on
To cover all my lines.

I got my purse out at reception
To pay for my admission
I was boastful to the cashier
'My boyfriend's a musician'.

'So is mine' she answered
'He plays the old trombone
When he starts to practise
I walk the streets alone'.

She said that once she knew a chap
Who played the clarinet
'They call themselves musicians?'
She hadn't met a good one yet.

D
a
v
e

I said 'well, mine's a drummer'
Her face turned to dismay
She said 'well, when you hear him
You'll want to run away'.

Then she boldly stated
'Don't forget to plug your ears
Or tinnitus will plague you
In your later years'.

How very true her words were
I should have heeded her kind warning
I go to pick my deaf aid up
First thing in the morning.

Brian

Lift — OUT OF ORDER

I went to a department store
To buy a birthday gift
I felt a proper wally
'Cause I got stuck in the lift.

I started yelling 'HELP!'
I really felt quite daft
I hoped someone would hear me
As it echoed down the shaft.

I've been here for a week now
No-one really cares
I've really learned my lesson
Next time I'll use the stairs.

Hitching a Ride

Old Mrs Smith, always
Made a great fuss
Every time that she got on the bus.

The conductor would call out 'Hold on Tight'
And she gripped the rail, with all of her might
She had leg muscles as strong as steel
But one day she rolled under the wheel.

Now when they meet out on the street
She reminds him that he caused her flat feet
He always says 'You know that I'm sorry'
Once he warned her 'Watch out, there's a lorry!'

Now poor Mrs Smith gets really tired
So a wheelchair has had to be hired
It's the conductor now, who makes all the fuss
As she hitches it up to the back of the bus.

Office Party

At last a quiet moment
I sit here reminiscing
Of the bawdy office party
Of my boss, who I was kissing.

I put my glass of wine down
And it just disappeared
I think that father Christmas
Hid it underneath his beard.

They were playing all the oldies
Like Knees up Mother Brown
We were giving it all that
We're now the talk of the town.

Every year's the same
My bosses P.A. Mable
Has to take her high heels off
And dance up on the table.

I've created an impression
So I'm keeping it low key
I don't want the office staff
Looking down on me.

We've got ten days off for Christmas
Then we'll be going back
I'll be a very lucky lady
If I don't get the sack.

The Day Trip

It's a lovely sunny morning
The sky is clear and blue
I said to my other half
"I know what we'll do".

"We'll drive down to the beach
It's really not too far
It shouldn't take too long
To get the stuff packed into the car.

I rustled up some sandwiches
And a flask of tea I made
And a bucket for sandcastles
With little Johnny's spade.

I put the swimming trunks and towel
In a nice neat pile
We'll be heading to the sea side
In just a little while.

We've got sunglasses and cameras
And tubes of suntan creams
And being extra cautious
Three spare pairs of jeans.

We cram into the car
With spare clothes, toys, the lot
And I've not forgotten
The baby's training pot.

The roads are very busy
They're queuing up for miles
It's taken away our eagerness
And wiped away our smiles.

Baby's getting grumpy
I bounce him on my knee
And Johnny's looking frumpy
He says he needs a wee.

We drive a little longer
It's further than I thought
My husband's lost his patience
I can tell he's looking fraught.

Finally we get there
And seek a place to park
A cloud's appeared from nowhere
And it's turned a little dark.

The baby needs his nappy changed
We're all gasping for a drink
Please will someone help me?
I'm almost on the brink.

We unpack the entire picnic
Guess what, it starts to rain
We sit there like four drowned rats
Then trudge back home again!

Wish You Were Here

Having a great time
Wish you were here
Smooching down the clubs all night
All tanked up with beer.

Went into a dive last night
Saw talented lap dancers
Could have had one in my room
But wasn't taking chances

I really am behaving well
I wouldn't let you down
Please send me some more money Mum
Gotta meet a blonde in town.

Your number one
Loving son.

Eye wisht eyed leernt to spell

Last year I started getting bored
Something was lacking in my life
Every day was so mundane
I was a typical housewife.

I'd tried my hand at knitting
The sort of things you learn at school
Knit one purl one slip one
I made a lovely shawl.

My house soon filled with pretty scarves
Edged with pom-poms or a fringe
The very sound of knitting needles now
Makes me want to cringe.

Then I tried my hand at painting
Cross hatching with a brush
I tried to sell some once
I'm still waiting for the rush.

The next thing I did was pottery
And got knee deep in clay
My family all laughed at me
So I threw it all away.

Then I had a go at cross-stitch
On a fourteen count of aida
My friend put in an order
She loved the piece I made her.

In my mind I had ambition
I was hell bent on succeeding
So I went down to the library
And got a book on beading.

My needles gone all crooked
And my threads got in a knot
What have I got to show for it?
Well, really not a lot.

I think I need new glasses
This may sound a bit absurd
But as I sit here writing this
My vision's getting blurred.

Here's a little secret
Just between you and me
I've entered for Poet Laureate
With my poetry.

I haven't got much chance of winning
Not a hope in hell
I was always bottom of the class
Eye wisht eyed leernt to spelll.

A Catastrophic Tail

Prunella the puss had a very fine tail
Of which she was very proud
Unfortunately something happened
Which caused her to squeal really loud.

She was about to enter the parlour
When a down draft blew in the door
It caught the tip of her tail
Which made it feel awfully sore.

The vet turned and said to Prunella
'You should have moved out of the way fast
You haven't left me an option
It will have to be set in a cast'.

Prunella winced at the vet
And curtly replied 'No Thanks'
I'll be happy for you to remove it
And I'll live the rest of my life as a Manx.

To Be Read Three Times a Day with a Glass of Wine

Every week I see my doctor
He says 'not you again'
Really my dear lady
You're becoming quite a pain.

I am so very sorry doctor
There are some things you should be told
I know you're going to tell me
It's because I'm getting old.

When I bend to put my slippers on
I pull a muscle in my back
Then my knee goes out of joint
It's vitamins I lack.

I've grown a wart upon my cheek
And my chin is getting hairy
I've thin tram lines around my neck
It's really getting scary.

When I put my lipstick on
I smudge it on my chin
Because my hand is shaking
And my lips are going thin.

When I take my bra off
My boobs droop on my belly
I'm a very close resemblance
To a Rowntrees moulded jelly

My hearing aid's minute
It's made up of micro-chips
But I still can't hear a word
I have to read your lips.

I meander round the shoe shops
And for my days of youth I mourn
As every shoe I try
Presses on my corn.

I can't eat in a hurry
Have to take my time and chew
Or else I get a stomach cramp
And end up on the loo

My teeth are like the stars
They all come out at night
I can't look in the mirror
'Cause I give myself a fright.

I've got pills for this and pills for that
Including constipation
Then I suffer from the side effects
With a massive palpitation.

When I sleep around my daughter's house
She shuts my bedroom door
Because I keep them up all night
With my reverberating snore.

They say I've lost my marbles
But I know that's not true
I've never played with marbles
I wouldn't have a clue.

Please don't mention the computer
Even worse is email
I don't understand a word of it
I'm just an ancient female.

They tell me if I 'log-on'
I can surf the net
Is it like the one they use
When my hair is set?

Lately I've put on some weight
It's probably water retention
I've started to float in the bath
Thought it was just worth a mention.

My wrists are feeling quite weak
It's probably osteoporosis
But I'll cross that off my list
I can't face the diagnosis.

The doctor turned and looked at me
Do you know what he said?
'You're lucky to be sitting here
By all accounts you should be dead'.

You need a medication
It's not been invented yet
I'm going to refer you
To go and see the vet.

So I got the yellow pages out
And rang the vet in town
He took one look at me and said
'I'm going to have to put you down'.

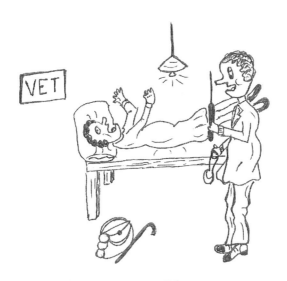

Farmed Out

I had a pain in my foot
Every time I walked
I had a pain in my jawbone
Every time I talked.

I had a pain in my neck
When I looked over my shoulder
My friends and I agree
It's because we're all getting older.

I take paracetamol and codeine
Sometimes something stronger
That's the price we have to pay
Because we're living longer.

When I'm walking to the shops
I can hear my tablets rattle
And when I see my doctor
We're all herded in like cattle.

I've sat and thought about it
There's not much we can do
But it really hurts my feelings
When they call me a 'silly moo'.

But it's only an expression
It won't do me any harm
The only time I'll worry
Is when they herd me to the farm.

Another Dilemma

I'd like to buy a magazine and give myself a treat
I'll make a cup of coffee and get a stool to raise my feet.

I search along the shelves to choose something to read
I don't want one with a free gift, there's nothing that I need.

I don't want one with recipes and the latest cookery tips
Or hints of exercises to shape my bulky hips.

I don't want to read about romances that have fell apart
How he found another partner and broke her little heart.

I don't want one with gardening hints to make my flowers
grow
Last year I bought 6 packets of seeds that I forgot to sow.

I don't care about disasters and how she saved his life
Or that when he regained consciousness he asked her to be
his wife.

Can you tell me why it is, I always see a pile
In my doctors' waiting room, they all look just my style?

They all look worse for wear with covers that are torn
All heaped in a ragged stack looking quite forlorn.

I don't care if they're ancient and really out of date
When the doctor calls me I always make him wait.

Do you think that they would miss one if I slipped it in my
bag?
I would willingly donate a pound, I've got to have this mag.

Decree Nisi

Hey diddle diddle
The cat kicked the fiddle
The cow ran away from the moon
The little dog howled
Cause he'd hurt himself
And the dish poked fun at the spoon
They all had a divorce, of course
Even nursery rhymes have to keep up with the times.

DIVORCE
CASE NUMBERS
1. CAT AND FIDDLE
2. COW AND MOON
3. DISH AND SPOON

ALL NON —
CONTESTED

Thursday Dawns

I find it very hard
To keep on top of all my tasks
So I engage someone to help me
She does everything I ask.

She visits every Thursday
To use a duster and a broom
And whizzes around the house
To tackle every room.

My house is not that bad
I could not live in dirt
She picks up clothes from the floor
Like trousers or a skirt.

Don't let me mislead you
It was clothes I'd had a 'try on'
I make myself more work
Cause now they'll need an iron.

She tackles all the cobwebs
Where I could never reach
And oversteps my budget
On disinfectant plus thick bleach.

She waltzes with the vacuum cleaner
Up and down the stairs
And when she cleans the dining room
Moves out all the chairs.

She wipes around the basin
And underneath the toilet seat
Then shines around the taps
And leaves the bathroom neat.

When she mops the kitchen tiles
You could eat from off the floor
Then cleans the greasy finger marks
From every cupboard door.

If she spies a piece of paper
It goes onto a pile
One day I will sort it out
And buy myself a file.

Every night I pray and thank God
She keeps my house so clean
I'm afraid that I will wake up
And my home-help was a dream.

Hip Hip Hooray

I had an accident one day
Missed a step and had a trip
Now I've just come out of hospital
With a brand new hip.

I'm now recuperating
And been told to exercise
I thought it would be simple
But was in for a surprise.

Today I used a wheelchair and learnt to steer myself
But all the merchandise I reached was from the lower shelf.

Brian was embarrassed; in fact he got quite lippy
He said I'd got to slow down, he thought I was too nippy.

Thank God I'd picked a day when Sainsbury's trade was quiet
If there'd been a few more customers I may have caused a
riot.

You just cannot imagine the freedom that I felt
But the names that I got called were just below the belt.

I learned to do a 3 point turn although it took me half an hour
I spun around so many times my yoghurts all turned sour.

Although this shopping trip was completely unplanned
I cannot for the life of me accept why I've been banned.

I'll have to hurry up and learn to walk again
So please pass me my crutches, oh the pain! The pain! The
pain!

Written 2004 after my hip replacement.

P.E. For O.A.P.s

Come on ladies stretch your toes
The gym will help you to forget your woes.

Skip up and down, it's good for your heart
Mrs Smith, keep your feet apart.

Oh My God she's fell on the floor
She's not doing badly though, for ninety-four.

I think she was doing an Irish jig
Her teeth fell out and she lost her wig.

Lately Mrs Hills has got thinner
She's forgotten how to cook a dinner.

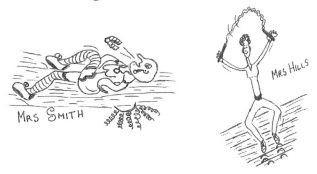

No Ivy! The backbends not for you
Watch out ladies there's a flying shoe!

Nora Simpson's head is reeling
She's just jumped up and hit the ceiling.

Who's that bouncing on her belly?
I should have known, it's rotund Nelly.

Maggie Brown's gone through the floor
She won't be coming anymore.

NELLY.

NORA SIMPSON

MAGGIE BROWN

She's just had a hip replacement
Now she's landed in the basement.

She doesn't hear a word I say
She lost her deaf aid yesterday.

It looks like all of the class has flopped
I wonder why the music's stopped.

Wait while I investigate
It means we'll run a little late.

Did I hear you chant you're tired?
You know how long this hall's been hired.

We can't afford to take the chance
We have to book it in advance.

We plan ahead at least a year
And hope and pray we're all still here.

Just chat and keep yourselves amused
It's probably the plug that's fused.

There, that's it, I've got in going
Heavens, Dora's tights need sewing.

Right now ladies, concentrate
We're running 20 minutes late.

Reach up ladies, to the sky
Heavens, Rose! Not that high.

You've pulled your shoulder out of joint
Will you ever get the point?

It seems our strength has now diminished
Well the class is almost finished.

Go straight home, don't try new tricks
And don't forget your walking sticks!

6.05. Special

Commuter express racing along the track
Wheels hurtling round clickety clack.

The suited gent with nodding head
Dreaming, wishing, he was still in bed

The model woman with heels so high
Watching commuters pushing by.

The lad in jeans and ear-ringed nose
Not caring really where he goes.

A school boy with his upturned collar
Looking like a serious scholar.

A lady with her head in a book
Now and again takes a hurried look
To see what station she is at
Subconciously adjusts her hat.

An OAP with his carrier bag
Lights a ciggie and takes a drag.

All different characters, all with one aim
Just to get off of this very fast train.

Pie in the Sky

What shall I cook for dinner tonight?
I fancy something quite tasty
I have some time to spare for a change
Usually I'm being quite hasty.

I'll take a look in my recipe book
It may give me some inspiration
What's this I spy? Oh duck a l'orange
And chicken au coronation.

Then I turn the page and see dressed jambon
All coated in Dijon mustard
Then afterwards for dessert course
They're suggesting meringue and crème custard.

On the next page, surprise surprise
Are lamb cutlets infused with mint jelly
Just like the ones a famous chef cooked
When he demonstrated on the telly.

Ah! This one looks good; it's pork in soy sauce
I imagine it tastes very scrummy
My mouth is beginning to water
And I'm getting a rumbly tummy.

Must hurry up and make up my mind
The time is beginning to fly
Or we'll be eating al fresco, from the deli at Tesco
Haute cuisine will be 'Pie in the Sky'.

Progress

Don't drink too much coffee
It contains too much caffeine
Don't eat chocolate late at night
It will only make you dream.

Don't eat that red tomato
It may be just a clone
And keep clear of the air waves
That are coming from your phone.

Don't eat fatty meat
Choose white meat nice and lean
And don't breathe in the fumes
Of leaded gasoline.

When you've had your fish and chips
You may feel a little sick
because the cod had just escaped
from an oil slick.

Our cabbage has been treated
To keep fresh about 5 years
And Ugli fruits, grown pretty now
To allay all our fears.

You can lower you cholesterol
If you stick to low fat spread
It smells just like gelatine
Granddad rubs onto his head.

If like me, you are short sighted
And you think it's getting worse
They can treat you with a laser beam
And you'll see things in reverse.

The latest washing powder
Will remove all signs of stain
It just dissolves the garment
But the buttons will remain.

You can dial up the plumber
To fix an urgent leak
But the answer-phone will tell you
'Please call back next week'.

Everything's organic now
We should all be going 'green'
Well that's okay I suppose
If you are a runner bean.

The computer's taken over
So it's email, www, dot com
And when you forget what day it is
Consult your cd rom.

We travel supersonic now
But there's more advance to come
Our dads will soon be giving birth
And we can call them mum.

Spend and Save

I need to get some shopping
I have just run out of tea
I cannot believe my luck
It is buy one get one free.

I spy a great big sponge cake
With a free carton of cream
The diet's out the window
Size 10 is just a dream.

Then I see some cheap bananas
As I push my trolley past
I must admit their overripe
We'll have to eat them fast.

Wow, a pack of toilet rolls
Enough to last a year
I'll warn the kids "Don't block the loo"
They will be wasteful though, I fear.

I know I've got a sweet tooth
I've grabbed four jars of honey
It is buy one get one free
I must be saving money.

Oh look, there's half price chicken legs
They will help fill a plate
But I'll have to cook them straight away
They're nearly out of date.

I should have made a shopping list
I knew I'd over spend
What's that? Cheap bleach over there,
That cleans round the U-bend.

I think I'll get some eggs
To make an omelette for a change
It will have to be the 'value' ones
I can't afford 'free-range'.

Somewhere I had a coupon
For half price low fat butter
I hope it's in my handbag
Amid this load of clutter.

Oh look inside that freezer
At those great lean beefy joints
I'll have to have a couple
Think of all the double points.

I'd better go and pay now
I can hardly push the trolley
Oh blast! It's started raining
I'll have to buy a brolley.

I really do hate shopping
It's an experience I dread
It's only when I've put it all away
I realise I've got no bread!

Laundered Money

I woke up this morning
As usual I was skint
Then I saw a job was vacant
At the royal mint.

How convenient I thought
A chance to make some money
Actually printing bank notes
Now doesn't that sound funny?

The application form arrived
It came by first class post
I answered all the questions
Well that is, nearly most.

You see I had worked in a laundry
Although I'd got the sack
I couldn't move the heavy bags
They really hurt my back.

They called me for an interview
But said 'we're sorry Sonny
You might get confused
And start to launder money'.

I said 'hang on a minute
That's not my basic plan
I'm trying to come clean
And be an honest man'.

They couldn't offer me the job
They're really being hard
But promised to consider me
If I produce an I.D. card.

Mail Shot Offers

Do I need a stair lift?
Or a walk in bath?
Do I need a hearing aid?
Please don't make me laugh.

Do I need a walking stick?
Or a walking frame?
Or pills to help my memory
Hang on, what's my name?

Do I need a gripper on a stick?
So I don't have to bend
Do I need equity release?
To give me cash to spend.

Do I need private health care?
In case I have a fall
All these mail shot offers
Just drive me up the wall.

Do I need a funeral plan?
To put my mind at ease
Do I need support tights?
For my arthritic knees.

All this is upsetting me
It's causing lots of tension
The only blasted thing I need
Is a higher retirement pension.

A Sticky Situation

Gerry worked in a factory
His job was stirring glue
One day he had the misfortune to trip on the lace of his shoe.

He went head first into the glue pot
The stuff just went everywhere
Gerry was deeply incensed
'Cause he had always been proud of his hair

That night when he went down the pub
All his mates yelled out 'Gerry, Crikey
There's no need to be so stuck up
Just 'cause your hairstyle is spiky'.

A Shining Example

Katrina was grooming her cat
As she always did lovingly
When to her absolute horror
Out hopped a frisky fat flea.

Katrina ran to the kitchen
Hunting the aerosol spray
She knew she had to be quick
Before Freddy the flea hopped away.

In her haste she grabbed the wrong can
In a panic to quickly abolish
And now the cat and flea
Have been sprayed and shone with polish!

Free?

I had a letter from my bank
Offering a special deal
And being as my funds were low
The offer did appeal.

It said 'You're credit rating's up
And so we've raised your limit'
Strange I thought my statement read
My account had nothing in it.

So I took the offer up
And made the FREE phone call
I could not believe my luck
I could go and have a ball.

They just lumped my debts together
Then put them on one card
I only had one monthly payment
That shouldn't be too hard.

Because I responded quickly
They sent me a FREE clock
It almost drove me mad
With it's flipping loud 'Tic-Toc'.

You see it just reminded me
I was living life on tick
I lay awake at night
The worry made me sick.

Then the payment day did dawn
I opened my purse to count
I never had an option
But to pay the least amount.

I've done this now for five long years
I can't get out of trouble
I only pay the interest
So my debt is almost double.

Then one sunny morning
I have the lord to thank
I had a special offer
From another high street bank.

It said 'Transfer your debts to us
Have six months interest FREE'
I thought this might be my last chance
To go on a spending spree.

I weighed up all my options
What had I got to lose?
And the thought of another FREE gift
Which I even got to choose.

So now I'm in debt forever
There are scores of people like me
Temptation is a terrible thing
When you are offered something FREE.

Published in the Daily Mail August 17th 2004

HELP

Community charge, electric bill
Oh go away, I do feel ill
Gas reminders, how I hate
I always seem to pay them late
The water rates are overdue
Oh well, that's nothing new
An immediate plan is needed here
If we want to survive another year
It's no good sitting in at home
I'll have to use the telephone
I comb my hair to look my best
I feel a proper toff
'Hello, is that the job centre?'
Oh No! My phone's cut off!

Justice Will Be Done

Sometimes I really get confused
The Law is blatantly abused
This account is all about
How a certain man, the law did flout.

This chap went speeding through the town
And inadvertently mowed a pedestrian down
As luck would have it someone saw
And rightfully informed the Law.

An Inspector was assigned to search for clues
Joined by a reporter from the 'weekly news'
They both were hopeful for the scoop of the year
Especially the Inspector, with promotion drawing near.

So an arrest and interview took place
The police were on a wild goose chase
'It wasn't me Guv, I was at 'ome
Rabbiting' on me dog 'n' bone".

"But someone noted your number plate
And your tax is out of date".

"Cross me 'eart I am a saviour
I did me mate a little favour
I know I took a bloomin' risk
I only lent him my tax disc.

Ya see we did a little deal
He promised me he wouldn't squeal
Ya see I bungled up a job
I was the leader of the mob.

Me jemmy touched the burglar alarm
Rebounded off and crushed his arm
Our mugs were snapped on CCTV
And all the gang are blaming me.

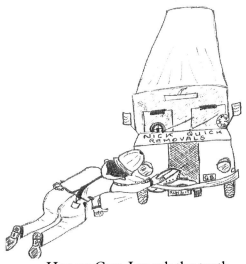

Honest Guv, I speak the truth
I know I look a bit uncouth"
"I'll just go out and check your tyres
I've met your type, you're expert liars.

What's this caught in your bumper?
It looks like a designer jumper?"
"Okay Guv, I must admit
I really didn't mean to hit.

They just stepped out in front of me
I didn't notice, didn't see
I was tuning in me radio
Wasn't sure which way to go.

Then I swerved to miss an arctic lorry
Honest Guv, I'm really sorry
Ya see I'm living on the brink
Trying to cut down on me drink.

I know I look a messy slob
I'm trying to find a decent job
Last year I had an interview
The form said we will contact you.

They ain't replied yet up to date
But sometimes my post is late
I know this sounds a bit absurd
But it's the truth Guv, every word.

If you charge me with this crime
You know it's all a waste of time
I think the Law's a load of bull
What's more, I know the prison's full.

I'd get twelve months and just serve three
Anyway it WASN'T ME"
"For the record this case is dismissed
You will be taken off the suspects list"
"Righto Guv, I'm warnin' ya, I'm gonna counter claim
For humiliatin' me and blackenin' my name.

Once I win me case and get me dosh safe in the bank
I'll say Hooray for British Justice, and have the taxpayer to
THANK!"